AFRICA'S BIG FIVE

SUNBIRD
PUBLISHING

First published 2001
2 4 6 8 10 9 7 5 3 1
Sunbird Publishing (Pty) Ltd
34 Sunset Avenue, Llandudno, Cape Town, South Africa
Registration number: 4850177827

Publisher Dick Wilkins
Editor Brenda Brickman
Designer Mandy McKay
Production Manager Andrew de Kock

Reproduction by Unifoto (Pty) Ltd, Cape Town
Printed and bound by Tien Wah Press (Pte) Ltd, Singapore

ISBN 0 62403 971 4

TITLE PAGE *In a breeding herd of elephants, cows and calves stay close together for protection, the bond between mother and daughter enduring for up to 50 years.*
LEFT *White rhinos need to drink every three or four days and a reliable source of water is essential for their wellbeing.*
BELOW *Lion cubs weigh a mere one to two kilograms at birth, and are kept well hidden by their mother until they are four to eight weeks old.*
OPPOSITE *Buffalo have a broad muzzle and their ears are large and fringed with hair.*

Africa's Big Five

The Big Five – an evocative term that fires the imagination – was coined not by rangers in an attempt to persuade travellers to visit Africa's game reserves, but by the 'great white hunters' of yesteryear to describe the most difficult and dangerous of the animals they hunted as trophies.

The giants of the African bush – the elephant, and the black and white rhinos – are also known as pachyderms, a term derived from the Greek word meaning 'thick skinned'.

The African elephant *(Loxodonta africana)* is the largest of these and, in fact, of all land animals, a mature bull elephant weighing as much as six tons. Huge amounts of food and water are needed to feed an animal this size; it is estimated that an adult can drink up to 200 litres of water, and eat up to

ABOVE When water is scarce elephants dig wells in dry riverbeds, using their trunks and front feet to reach the water that seeps through the sand.

BELOW A cow, alerted to possible danger to her calf, raises her head and spreads her ears, appearing larger and more threatening.

250 kilograms of grass, leaves and bark a day. In the elephants' daily search for sufficient food and clean water, the herd will traverse many kilometres, often wreaking havoc on the vegetation that lies in their path, stripping trees of their branches and bark and even pushing them over to reach the sweeter shoots that burst only from the topmost branches.

In the dry season, elephants cover even greater distances in their search for liquid replenishment, and as large herds congregate to drink at water holes and pans, individuals jostle for space and bad-tempered bulls clash with one another.

Elephant herds vary greatly in size, from small groups of just a few animals to large herds of over 100. Herds are led by a matriarch, usually the oldest cow in the group, and consist of cows of different ages and their offspring. Once a male elephant has reached puberty he moves away from the matriarchal herd, and usually remains solitary, although he may join up in a temporary social arrangement with another herd. Sometimes a young bull will befriend an older male, one that will teach the newcomer the ways of the bush, but even very sociable bulls will not stay together for very long.

Elephant cows breed throughout the year and a bull wandering into a matriarchal herd will almost certainly check whether any are in oestrus. Bulls in musth, which is a state of heightened sexual agitation, are extremely aggressive towards other males (and everything in general) and are carefully avoided by other elephants.

After a gestation period of 22 months, a cow will give birth to a calf weighing some 120 kilograms. The calf spends its first few months safely tucked under its mother's belly, suckling from the breasts situated between her front legs, running along underneath her or right next to her as she moves with the herd. A calf is dependent on its mother for up to two years, and during this time several females in the herd will share any babysitting responsibilities.

Family units are tight-knit groups and a breeding herd of elephants will aggressively defend its young.

Male and female calves show distinct differences in character. Male youngsters are far more unruly than their sisters. Both sexes, however, love to wallow and play in the water and the thick oozy mud found at water holes and pans, shoving and clambering over each other, squealing and trumpeting in delight. If play becomes too raucous an adult elephant will intervene to bring the herd's offspring under control.

Just as elephants wallow, not only to keep cool but also to cover themselves in a layer of mud that provides relief from irritating parasites and the harsh African sun, so too do their fellow pachyderms, the

ABOVE A black rhino calf runs behind or next to its mother. Should they be separated, they will call to one another in high-pitched squeaks and squeals.

white rhinoceros *(Ceratotherium simum)* and the black rhinoceros *(Diceros bicornis)*. The two rhino species have easily identifiable differences, the most obvious being the shape of the head and lips. The white rhino has a longer head with a square-shaped muzzle ideal for grazing short grass, while the black has a tapering muzzle with a prehensile or hooked upper lip that enables it to browse on the leaves of trees. The word 'white' is a misnomer and does not refer to the white rhino's colour, which is grey, but rather to the shape of its lips, and is derived from the Dutch word *wijd* – meaning wide.

Both species have very poor eyesight but an excellent sense of hearing and smell.

Rhinos make full use of the red-billed oxpeckers that feast off the parasites on their thick hides, also using these birds as an early warning system to alert them to imminent danger.

Both black and white rhinos have horns made of tightly compressed hair-like filaments, which are attached to the skin rather than to the bone. The front horn of the white rhino is usually much longer than the back one, while in the black rhino the difference is less marked.

ABOVE *The white rhino has a square lip that is ideally suited to grazing short grass.*

White rhinos give birth throughout the year and, after a gestation period of about 16 months, a calf weighing about 40 kilograms is born. The calf will begin to graze after about one week, and is dependent on its mother for its first year, during which time she will fiercely defend it against any danger. As they move through the bush, the youngster runs in front of its mother, who guides it with her horn. The bond between mother and calf is strong, and family units of a cow with offspring of varying ages are often encountered.

In contrast, the black rhino is a solitary, irascible animal with no fixed territory and a penchant to charge at the slightest provocation. It is also grey in colour but darker and smaller than the white rhino, an adult bull weighing about 1.1 tons. Black rhino bulls also spray-urinate and leave middens, but this is to announce their presence rather than to demarcate territory.

It is unusual for individuals to form associations, and bulls actually appear to make every effort to avoid each other, confrontations therefore being rare among them. However, in the presence of a female in oestrus, rival males will fight violently in competition for her favours, and this can result in serious injury and even death to at least one of them.

The gestation period is about 15 months and a single calf is born weighing around 40 kilograms. The

The white rhino is the larger animal, an adult bull weighing some 2.3 tons. It is more placid and sociable, occurring in groups of between two and five animals led by a dominant bull. His territory varies in size from one to five square kilometres and he marks off his area by strategically placed latrines or middens, and by spray-urinating along the boundaries. The bull will tolerate the presence of a number of subordinate males in and around his terrain and allows easy access to visiting cows and their calves, which move through the territories of several bulls in their foraging. However, should another dominant bull wander into his domain, fierce fighting may ensue, especially if a resident female is in oestrus, and these confrontations sometimes result in death.

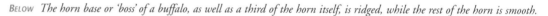

BELOW *The horn base or 'boss' of a buffalo, as well as a third of the horn itself, is ridged, while the rest of the horn is smooth.*

calf is able to walk and suckle after about three hours, and runs alongside or behind its mother. Unlike the white rhino, the black rhino cow rejects her youngster when she falls pregnant again, or when her next calf is born, which is about once every three years.

Calves from both species sometimes fall prey to lions and hyenas, but in many cases the cow manages to defend her young against these predators. Rhinos have little contact with most other mammals, but black rhinos can be particularly cantankerous when competing for water, and will not only squabble with others of their kind at water holes and pans but also with elephants and buffalo.

African buffalo *(Syncerus caffer)* usually gather around water points in the early morning and the late afternoon. They are gregarious animals, occurring in large herds that can number several thousand in the dry season. It is common for smaller groups and bachelor herds to move off from the large herd, only to rejoin it at a later stage. Lone bulls are often encountered and have a reputation for being bad-tempered and irritable, especially if wounded or sick.

Hunters, past and present, give these animals a wide berth, as they can be cunning and unpredictable, seeking out and charging the perceived cause of their pain. In contrast a herd of buffalo is normally quite placid, retreating into the shade to lie up during the heat of the day, to mill about, chew the cud or wallow in the mud. Should they become alarmed, however, the whole herd may stampede together, crashing and snorting through the bush, the mass of panicked animals presenting a formidable sight.

Buffalo usually feed during the night and in the early morning, preferring lush valleys, open grasslands and savanna bushveld. Large herds of feeding and drinking buffalo inadvertently help other grazers as they trample

ABOVE A buffalo herd has a clearly defined range in which abundant grass, water and shade are essential.

down the old undergrowth, encouraging the new growth to come through.

Cattle-like in appearance, adults are dark brown to black in colour, while calves are a reddish brown. An adult male buffalo can weigh as much as 700 kilograms. They have characteristically huge horns, used for fighting and protection, which curve upward from a base or 'boss' that joins the horns over the forehead. The boss is exceptionally well developed in the bulls, to a lesser extent in the cows, and is absent in the calves.

Within the herd, both bulls and cows have a definite hierarchy and the dominant males will mate with the females that are in season. After a gestation period of about 340 days, a cow will give birth to a calf, which weighs around 40 kilograms.

Calves are usually born during the summer months, when the grass is at its most nutritious.

A buffalo cow does not move off to give birth but stays with the herd and within a few hours the calf is able to walk.

During this period, when the youngster is still trying to find its feet, and afterwards during its early years, it is vulnerable to predation by lions and hyenas, and it is estimated that four out of every 10 calves do not reach maturity.

The mother will aggressively defend her offspring, and her calf will stay with her for approximately two years. When threatened a herd will, on occasion, close ranks, the bulls encircling the cows and calves, presenting a nearly impenetrable front to the enemy. Buffalo are largely intolerant of lions, and will charge to scare them off, lowering their massive heads to inflict maximum injury with their formidable horns.

BELOW   An adult male lion usually sports a full mane, which covers the sides of his face and extends down onto his neck, chest and shoulders.

The lion *(Panthera leo)*, often called the king of the beasts, is the largest African cat, and an adult male can weigh as much as 240 kilograms. Lions are sociable animals and occur in family groups or prides, the size of which varies from five to 12 or more.

Prides rest up in the heat of the day, and during these periods members loll around together in the shade, and it is quite common for different individuals to mimic another's behaviour, yawning, grooming or scratching in turn. During this time they conserve their energy for the hunt, which is usually conducted under cover of darkness by the females in the pride. These quiet periods are also used by pride members to renew their social bonds, as hunting and feeding are violent affairs.

The lion's prey ranges from porcupine to antelope, from buffalo to giraffe. While the lionesses do most of the work, adult males usually assist when their brute strength is needed to bring down an especially large animal. At a kill, the males will feed first, followed by the females and then the cubs; fighting and squabbling around the carcass continues until there is nothing left to eat. Any slow or timid cubs will go hungry, and they soon learn to tussle for their share of the meat.

Lions reach their prime at about five years of age, and at this time they are particularly aggressive, fighting not only for territorial dominance but also for dominance over the females in the pride.

Single males form coalitions in order to improve their chances of holding a pride's territory, which can cover vast areas depending on the availability of prey. The new dominant males will often kill the cubs of the previously dominant males, forcing the females into season and, after intense mating, most lionesses within the pride conceive and give birth at the same time.

ABOVE   Lion cubs are weaned at the age of seven to 10 months. A lactating lioness will suckle any of the pride's cubs.

A female may mate with several males while she is in oestrus and as a result produce a litter where the cubs have different fathers.

Either the male or the female initiates mating and during this period the male stays close to the female, copulating every 15 minutes over several days. After a gestation period of about four months the lioness leaves the pride to give birth. Litters average two to four cubs.

The youngsters are dependent on their mother for almost two years, and it is only after two or even three years that they have sufficient skill to participate in a hunt. The cubs stay close to the pride for protection, and if separated from the rest they are vulnerable to predation, mainly by hyenas, but also by lions from other prides, and even by leopards.

The leopard (*Panthera pardus*) is a solitary animal and although smaller than the lion – an adult male weighing, at most, 90 kilograms – is regarded by many as the champion of the bush. Its coat is tawny in colour, dotted with dark rosettes that break up the outline of its body, enabling it to almost completely disappear against a dappled background.

The leopard is a skilled and intelligent hunter, hunting successfully on its own, and usually at night. Its diet varies from medium-sized antelope such as impala, duiker and bushbuck, to hares, rodents and even carrion.

If a leopard believes its kill is at risk of being snatched by other predators, it will quickly drag it up a tree, this being indicative of its strength, as an adult impala can weigh as much as 70 kilograms.

Leopards appear to have an inborn ability to hunt, as the young may accompany their mother on a hunt at only nine months of age, and, by the age of 11 months, have the ability to kill an impala or other similar-sized antelope.

Males effectively keep other males out of their territories by patrolling nightly, scent-marking the boundaries by spray-urinating and ground-scraping, Confrontation between males is uncommon, and, when it does occur, often results in death.

Females also scent-mark their territories, but not as diligently as their male counterparts, as they invariably have youngsters to feed and care for.

Although fighting between females does occur, it rarely proves fatal and they too prefer to avoid confrontation. In fact, it is only when they have the urge to mate that leopards will seek one another out, and this is particularly true in the case of the female, who will initiate the coupling.

Copulation takes place around every 15 minutes over a period of about four days, after which each cat will once again go its separate way. There is a gestation period of three and a half months, after which the female gives birth to one to three cubs, which she hides away in a secluded spot for a period of about six weeks.

The young are at this time particularly vulnerable to passing predators such as hyenas and lions, especially when she is forced to leave the cubs on their own when she goes off hunting.

The cubs are dependent on their mother for up to a year and become independent at the age of 18 months when, as young adults, they too begin to prefer their own company, leaving her to make their own way through the African bush.

BELOW *The leopard is sturdily built, with an elongated body and stocky legs. It has a wide head with powerful jaws, a long tail and strong curved claws.*

ELEPHANT

The African elephant is the largest land mammal in the world. Its distinguishing features, apart from its huge bulk, are its trunk, which is as dexterous as a pair of hands, large ears that cool the body when flapped, and tusks, which are actually elongated upper incisors. The elephant has poor eyesight but an acute sense of hearing and a superb sense of smell; it raises its trunk like a periscope to test for scents carried on the breeze. Elephants trumpet and 'scream' when angry, and otherwise communicate with one another in a series of deep rumblings. They also transmit information via infrasound, and a herd of noisy elephants will, as one, become absolutely still if they feel uneasy — a silent message passing between them.

LEFT From an early age male elephants use trunk-wrestling, shoving and sparring to establish dominance. These contests continue into early adulthood and assist young bulls in assessing their opponents' strength and fighting capabilities.

OPPOSITE Bull elephants leave the herd at about 12 years of age, and wander off on their own or join up with other bulls to form a bachelor herd, which usually includes males of varying ages.

LEFT Elephants are active both in the day and at night, but usually rest up in the shade during the heat of the afternoon. Herds will commonly make their way to water holes and pans for a drink and a bathe in the late afternoon.

BELOW Herds often move in single file, and at a steady pace, especially at night. Once on the move, they can cover vast distances, wearing paths across the landscape that they continue to use over many years.

OPPOSITE Elephants graze and browse, and spend a large proportion of their waking hours feeding. Their diet is varied, although they do show preferences for particular plant species, and will often cover long distances to get to their favourite food. During the rainy season they favour a variety of green grasses, which they uproot by coiling their trunks around the shoots.

THIS PAGE AND OPPOSITE The most curious of the elephant's features is its trunk, which is a combination of its upper lip and nose. When individuals greet one another they do so by intertwining their trunks and putting their trunk tips into one another's mouths. The trunk is multifunctional, and is used to smell, suck up water, pluck grass, and strip bark, leaves and branches from trees. An adult elephant's trunk is a heavy appendage, and the animal will sometimes drape it across its tusks to relieve the weight. Even when submerged in water, the elephant can use its sensitive trunk to probe for grasses in the mud underfoot.

PREVIOUS PAGE LEFT It is not unusual to see small family groups and lone bulls congregating at water sources; once they have quenched their thirst, they will usually move off alone or within the group, as they arrived.

PREVIOUS PAGE RIGHT Elephants are gregarious by nature and gather together to feed and drink. Large herds can devastate the surrounding vegetation during feeding, but, ironically, their dung can benefit the environment by providing the medium for the germination of certain seeds.

LEFT Elephants love water and when they come upon it, whether it be every day or, in drier areas, every third or fourth day, they will habitually bathe and wallow.

ABOVE Elephants use their trunks to draw up water and mud and, in a flicking motion, wet their backs and legs. After this ritual, they invariably give themselves a dust bath.

OPPOSITE The layer of mud that coats the elephants' bodies after a mud bath offers some relief from irritating flies and parasites, and also cools the animals down, at the same time providing protection from the harsh African sun.

LEFT African elephants have a wide variety of habitats, ranging from woodland to thick bushveld, and open grasslands to desert areas.

ABOVE The desert elephants found in Kaokoland, Namibia, are highly mobile and adaptable. They cover vast distances in the search for food and water, taking full advantage of the region's meagre rainfall.

OPPOSITE A reliable supply of water, sufficient vegetation for grazing and browsing, and shade in which to shelter during the heat of the day are essential prerequisites for the survival of elephant populations.

OVERLEAF LEFT Elephants drink huge amounts of water and it is estimated that an adult bull can consume up to 200 litres a day. They are capable of sucking up nine litres of water at a time.

OVERLEAF RIGHT Once the elephants have slaked their thirst, and, if the water is deep enough, they will wade into its depths to lie down, roll over or completely submerge themselves, with every evidence of pleasure.

LEFT AND OPPOSITE The bond between an mother elephant and her offspring is strong. Females are devoted to protecting and assisting their calves until they are old enough to fend for themselves.

TOP A calf suckles from its mother for two to three years and should she for some reason die during this time, another nursing female will adopt the young elephant.

ABOVE A baby elephant is unable to use its trunk effectively for the first six months of its life, and will only master the trunk's various uses as it matures.

LION

The lion is not only the largest African cat, but it is also the most sociable. Individuals live together in prides, the lionesses forming the nucleus of the group. Pride members hunt and feed together, and loll around in the shade in the heat of the day. While resting they groom themselves and one another. Females produce cubs every two years, quite frequently in synchrony. Males, in spite of their fearsome appearance and reputation, are surprisingly tolerant of playful cubs. Lions are territorial and, with few exceptions, the females will spend most of their lives within their own home ranges, rarely moving out of their domain.

LEFT Males feed first at a kill, the lionesses and cubs waiting their turn. A male can eat as much as 25 per cent of his own body weight, and large lions assume prime position at a carcass by virtue of their superior strength.

OPPOSITE Most hunting takes place during the night, although some hunts are made during the early morning and late afternoon. Commonly, the lionesses of a pride make the most kills, and they are usually alert to the presence of any potential prey.

LEFT Lions are opportunistic hunters and keep a sharp lookout for young, sick or injured animals that would increase the chance of a successful kill.

ABOVE The tawny colour of the lions' coats provides excellent camouflage in the dry grass of winter, but even during the rainy months, when the veld is green, a pride still manages to fade into the background.

OPPOSITE A large adult lion can weigh as much as 240 kilograms, and his brute strength and body weight go a long way in helping the animal to bring down larger prey such as buffalo and giraffe.

OVERLEAF LEFT When food is plentiful, lions will eat fairly peacefully with only minor squabbles breaking out around the kill; but when food is scarce and the pride is really hungry, violent confrontations over the prey can take place.

OVERLEAF RIGHT Lions avail themselves of any opportunity to eat, and an elephant carcass will provide food for days. The lions will stay in the vicinity of a carcass for some time and will continue to eat at the animal, even if the meat is in the process of putrefaction.

LEFT During the heat of the day, lions rest up in the shade under the trees, in thickets or reed beds. They are often bothered by flies, which they tolerate, up to a point, eventually snapping at them in irritation. If this does not have the desired effect, the lion will overcome its lethargy and move to another spot.

ABOVE It is estimated that lions doze and sleep for about 15 hours each day. During these rest periods, they loll around, lying on their sides, on their bellies and on their backs with their legs spread open.

OPPOSITE Lions are very sociable animals and the pride uses quiet periods to renew any bonds that the previous night's feeding might have undone. Mutual grooming is particularly effective in promoting the ties between members, and in this regard the lion's rough tongue is a competent tool.

OVERLEAF LEFT Lions are excellent stalkers and use any available cover to close in on their intended victims. When stalking, they keep their heads and bodies near to the ground and fix their eyes on the animal, moving slowly and intently towards it. If the prey shows signs of unease the lions will freeze, continuing only when the other animal relaxes.

OVERLEAF RIGHT In spite of its superior strength, the lion is particularly vulnerable to the porcupine, whose quills can pierce its flesh and cause festering that sometimes leads to a fatal infection.

LEFT Lions are territorial, and the size of their home range is largely dependent on the availability of game. Both males and females fiercely defend their territory against trespassing lions.

ABOVE A resident pride regularly patrols its domain and clearly marks territorial boundaries by spraying urine on the bushes, scratching the ground, and creating latrine sites. The roars of the male lion, audible over several kilometres, also serve to advertise to others that the area is occupied.

OPPOSITE It is not uncommon for lions, immediately after a successful kill, to roar loudly, the sound fading to a series of harsh grunts. They have a robust digestive system, the food passing through the stomach very quickly, which means they are able to eat again not long after gorging themselves.

OVERLEAF LEFT Having eaten its fill, a lion may conveniently fall asleep right on the carcass, as it waits for its metabolism to digest the food before it starts to feed again.

OVERLEAF RIGHT Lion cubs have ochre-coloured rosettes and spots on their haunches and legs, and sport a dark stripe down the centre of their backs. The cub's pelt is woollier than that of an adult, and for some time it will lack the characteristic tuft at the end of its tail.

ABOVE Lion cub mortality is high, increasing when times are hard and food is scarce, specifically when adults are forced to cover long distances to obtain food, and weakened cubs die of starvation or abandonment.

RIGHT Lions may eat their kill at the spot where the prey was brought down, or they may drag it to the nearest cover. They usually open the belly first and then draw out the stomach and intestines. Often the intestines are eaten after being pulled across the incisors, squeezing out the contents.

OPPOSITE Lions, including weaned cubs, will drink regularly when water is available, especially after feeding. They are, however, not dependent on water, and can go for long periods without drinking, obtaining their moisture from the blood of their prey.

RHINO

Although both African rhino species have a common ancestor, there are several fundamental differences between the two, including size, temperament, the shape of the muzzle and lips, and food preferences. Both, however, have been ruthlessly hunted and poached by man over the years for the sake of their horns, which are highly prized in the Far East, where they are ground into a powder that is used as an aphrodisiac, and in Yemen, where the horns are carved into dagger handles. As a result of successful conservation initiatives, the white or square-lipped rhino has staged a remarkable recovery, although the black or hook-lipped rhino remains an endangered species. At present, it appears that the best chance of survival for both breeds is in southern Africa, and more particularly in South Africa.

LEFT The white rhino is distinguishable from its black cousin by its square-shaped lips and the large hump on its neck. The hump is clearly evident when the animal lifts its head, which it usually carries close to the ground. The thick skin is folded at the shoulders, at the top of the front legs, and where the hind legs join the body.
OPPOSITE White rhinos occur in small groups, numbering between two and five animals, and these may consist of a dominant bull, subordinate bulls, cows and their offspring. Larger groups of up to 10 animals sometimes come together for short periods of time.

LEFT White rhinos are grazers, showing a preference for areas that provide short grasses. As they feed they walk slowly forward. They usually eat in the early morning and in the late afternoon, when it is relatively cool, but they are also active at night.

ABOVE A reliable source of drinking water is essential and each rhino family group has its favourite watering place. They often follow the same paths to water holes and pans, creating deeply grooved tracks. A rhino needs to drink regularly, which it does in the late afternoon and after sundown. During dry periods it will drink every two to three days.

OPPOSITE The rhino employs birds such as the pied crow and the red-billed oxpecker to rid itself of irritating ticks and other parasites that attach themselves to its thick hide. Fork-tailed drongos often swoop along the sides of resting rhinos to catch any hovering insects.

OVERLEAF LEFT During the heat of the day the rhino retreats to the shade where it sleeps, lying on its side or on its belly, with its large, ponderous head resting on the ground. Even during repose it has an excellent sense of hearing, but it also relies on birds, especially the ever-present red-billed oxpeckers, to warn it of any approaching danger.

OVERLEAF RIGHT A dominant bull has a clearly defined territory, which it defends against other males. Usually, trespassing bulls try to avoid confrontations, but should these occur then fierce fighting ensues, especially if a female on heat is present. Severe wounds can be caused by the horns, and ramming one another with their shoulders can lead to internal injury and even the death of one or both of the rhinos.

OVERLEAF LEFT The white rhino has trumpet-shaped ears that move independently of each other, and constantly rotate in an effort to pick up any strange sounds. The length of the horns is not determined by the animal's sex, and both male and female can sport substantial front horns.

OVERLEAF RIGHT A cow usually moves away from the group to give birth, and remains separated, with her calf, for several days. The calf suckles from its mother for about a year and during this time – at about four months and again at about 10 months – it moults its outer horny layer of skin.

ABOVE A rhino cow's home range overlaps that of other females and territorial bulls. Her terrain increases according to grazing and water availability.

RIGHT During the summer months, rhinos wallow in the mud or lie in shallow pools. This not only assists in regulating body temperature, but covers the body with a layer of mud, which, when it falls off, helps rid the animal of parasites. Terrapins may also feast on ticks while the rhino is wallowing.

OPPOSITE After mud wallowing the rhino will rub itself against trees and large rocks, which eventually become smooth and polished with constant use.

LEFT The black rhino is solitary and shy. When alarmed it can exhibit considerable aggression, and will give several snorts prior to charging. In spite of its size and weight, it is remarkably agile and can cover considerable distance at speed and turn on the spot.

BELOW Unlike the white rhino, the black rhino is a browser and has a prehensile upper lip to assist it in feeding. It has a shorter head, longer neck and smaller ears, and holds its head higher than its white counterpart.

OPPOSITE The prehensile or hooked lip is ideal for grasping twigs and shoots, which the black rhino snaps off or cuts with its premolars. It is selective in its choice of food and does not particularly like dry plant matter. It will sometimes eat grass during the rainy season.

ABOVE The black rhino requires a habitat that has trees and shrubs to a height of about four metres, with dense thickets in which to shelter from the heat.

ABOVE RIGHT Rhinos usually drink once a day, at sundown or at night.

OPPOSITE The black rhino is unsociable and associations between adults are temporary. However, the bond between a mother and her offspring, at least until the birth of her next calf, is strong, and she will fiercely defend her young against danger.

LEOPARD

The leopard is the quintessential cat — sleek, powerful, elusive and very independent. Physically smaller than its cousin, the lion, it has a formidable reputation as an expert hunter. A leopard is rarely seen in the company of others of its kind, except during the mating season or when a female is accompanied by her cubs. Its solitary nature means that it must, of necessity, be completely self-sufficient, and the leopard has an inherent ability to do this, aided by its exceptional senses of sight and hearing, and its cunning nature. Strangely contradictory, it will boldly hunt down prey more than twice its body weight, but will timidly take refuge up a tree when challenged by other predators.

LEFT While essentially terrestrial animals, leopards are at home in trees and are expert climbers, their sharp, powerful claws being ideal for grip and leverage. The elevated height of a tree provides an excellent lookout for potential prey and, during the heat of the day, a place to catch a cooling breeze.

OPPOSITE In spite of first appearances, no two leopards are alike. In general, they have dark spots on their legs, shoulders and heads, with rosettes covering the remainder of the body. The whiskers are long and white and evenly grouped in rows on the sides of the muzzle.

LEFT A leopard usually spends the day resting, lying up in a dense, shady thicket, on a rocky outcrop, or in the branches of a tree, particularly one into which it has dragged its kill.

BELOW A leopard may kill more than it immediately requires to survive. However, it will not necessarily stir to hunt again when evening falls, even if food sources are abundant.

OPPOSITE The leopard has exceptionally well-developed senses, particularly of sight and hearing. It will make full use of lofty perches from which to survey the surrounds and utilise these senses to locate a possible victim.

OVERLEAF LEFT The distinctive curve of the leopard's tail is often the first indication of its presence in a tree.

OVERLEAF RIGHT Secretive and solitary animals, leopards only emerge from dense cover for brief periods. In the early morning they are most often seen lying in the sun on rocky outcrops, and in the late afternoons, when they begin to stir for the evening hunt, they can be seen on the banks of rivers, exploring the rocks and vegetation.

LEFT The spots and rosettes on the leopard's tawny coat blend in with its surroundings by breaking up the outline of its body, enabling it to observe its enemies or potential prey without being seen itself.

ABOVE Leopard cubs are left behind by their mother when she goes on a hunt and during this time it is in the cubs' own interests to remain concealed and quiet, as sounds and movement attract predators and disturb possible prey. Invariably, however, they leap and bound about without fear.

OPPOSITE A mother leads her cubs, between the ages of about three and nine months, to a kill. When they are slightly older they may accompany her on a hunt, and by the age of 11 months are sufficiently skilled to make their own kill of an impala or similar-sized antelope. A mother and her cubs have a range of contact calls, and she summons them with abrupt purring sounds.

LEFT The presence of a hyena at the base of a tree is a sure sign that a leopard has made a kill and has hoisted it into the branches above.

TOP While the leopard eats, chunks of meat fall off the carcass onto the ground and will be quickly devoured by the scavenger below.

ABOVE After making a kill a leopard may drag the carcass to a sheltered spot to feed on it.

OPPOSITE Between feeds, the leopard will snooze, its prey safely stored alongside.

ABOVE When moving through long grass, a mother with cubs curves her tail upwards to reveal its white tip, which acts as a beacon for her young to follow, as often, playfully distracted, they need to hurry to keep up with her.

ABOVE Leopards are largely silent animals, but they do give a characteristic, rasping 'cough', especially males. These calls are usually made after nightfall and before dawn, when they are patrolling their territories.

ABOVE Leopards move slowly and stealthily and are constantly on the lookout for easy prey. Small victims such as mice and birds, which hide up in the long grass, are pounced on and swatted, and eaten on the spot.

ABOVE Leopards are shy and non-confrontational, and, if disturbed or alarmed, will instantly bound away, either slipping into the cover of the nearest bush, disappearing from view within seconds, or seeking refuge up a tree.

LEFT An older leopard may lose the full use of its teeth as they become worn down or broken off with constant use.

TOP Leopards stalk and pounce on prey, killing the animal by means of suffocation.

ABOVE Both males and females are territorial, and males in particular scent-mark boundaries by scratching on trees, scraping the ground and spray-urinating.

OPPOSITE The long whiskers and the extra-long hairs in the eyebrows are sensory, helping the leopard to avoid walking into obstacles at night.

OVERLEAF LEFT A leopard's claws can measure 30 millimetres across the curve.

OVERLEAF RIGHT Although a leopard does not need to drink regularly, it will, when water is available, drink readily.

LEFT A young leopard plays constantly, climbing trees, jumping from branch to branch, leaping and tumbling in the grass. These activities hone its skills for the time when, at the age of a year, it is no longer dependent on its mother, and will be able to hunt and fend for itself.

ABOVE Because of its solitary way of life and its ability to survive on a variety of food in environments ranging from forest to savanna, and even semidesert areas, the leopard is the most widespread of the larger predators in Africa.

OPPOSITE A mother leopard will fiercely defend her young from any danger; even so, cub mortality is high, and it is seldom that an entire litter survives to adulthood.

BUFFALO

The buffalo is perhaps the most misunderstood of Africa's Big Five, with a reputation for being bad tempered and highly dangerous. While this may be true of lone or wounded animals, a herd is usually quite placid, and, for the most part, almost cattle-like in demeanor. The buffalo is a massive animal, characterised by huge curved horns that meet over the forehead. Gregarious by nature, buffalo retreat into the shade in the heat of the midday sun, to mill about and chew the cud. Perhaps the most dangerous aspect about a herd is its tendency to stampede en masse when alarmed, snorting and crashing through the bush. A constant battle rages between the buffalo and its most notable natural enemy, the lion.

LEFT Large buffalo herds, numbering several thousand animals, are common during the dry season. In the wetter months, when food and water are more plentiful, the herd will split up into smaller groups.

OPPOSITE Buffalo herds have clearly defined home ranges, the size of which is determined by the amount of food and water available. They usually drink water in the early morning and again in the evening, and tend to graze near water, often resting in the shelter of the reed beds.

LEFT During the heat of the day, buffalo regularly wallow in the mud, which helps to control their body temperature, although not as efficiently as the shade into which the herd retreats when the sun is at its hottest.

BELOW Sensitive to heat, a buffalo will also lie up in shallow water in an attempt to keep cool when its body temperature rises uncomfortably.

OPPOSITE Buffalo bulls wallow far more frequently than cows, while the calves do so very rarely, if at all. The bulls will turn every which way in an attempt to coat as much of their bodies in mud as possible, including their faces and horns.

THIS PAGE AND OPPOSITE The red-billed oxpecker feeds on the ticks and blood-sucking flies that plague the buffalo. The oxpecker scrambles about on the hide of the animal in search of food, with little evidence of any objection from the buffalo, and, along with its rarer cousin, the yellow-billed oxpecker, usually stays out of sight on the far side of its host. If the buffalo is tolerant, however, the birds will explore for parasites around the eyes, ears and nose, and even in the mid-line of the horn base. The birds also serve as an early warning system for the animal, flying off with shrill twitters if they are alarmed.

ABOVE The thick layer of mud covering the hide of wallowing buffalo not only protects them from the harsh African sun but also provides some relief from the irritating ticks and other parasites the ever-present oxpeckers may have overlooked.

ABOVE The coating of mud that a buffalo rubs off against trees or boulders also helps in removing any parasites encrusted in the muddy layer.

ABOVE Low-lying branches and rough bark make useful surfaces against which to scratch any out-of-the way itches caused by biting flies and ticks.

OPPOSITE The hierarchy among the males in a smaller buffalo herd is maintained with threat displays, which include holding the head up high and showing off the length of the body. This may be accompanied by tossing of the head, and hooking motions made with the horns. If fighting does take place, rivals charge towards each other with heads and noses held forward, often grunting in the process. Before crashing into each other, they lower their heads to take the impact on the boss. This behaviour, is also evident in the females, but to a lesser extent.

OVERLEAF Buffalo herds are selective feeders during the wet season, but less so during the drier months, when they spend more time ruminating due to the higher fibre content of the food. While they predominately graze, they will occasionally browse.

ABOVE Although buffalo are gregarious animals, a lone animal that wanders into the home range of another herd will not be accepted, and will be chased off. Buffalo herd members have a variety of calls for different situations, including signals to move to water, to reassure the herd that all is well, or to alert the herd to the presence of danger.

RIGHT Buffalo are seasonal breeders and most calves are born during the warm summer months. The cow does not move away to give birth, but stays with the herd, and most births occur when the group is resting. A mother will sometimes leave her newborn calf in thick bush when she moves away to feed, and a calf that has lost sight of its mother will bleat anxiously until she answers with a croaking call.